Dear I

A Feminis
in Fifteen

Also by Chimamanda Ngozi Adichie

Dear Ijeawele,

or
A Feminist Manifesto in Fifteen Suggestions

Chimamanda Ngozi Adichie

4th ESTATE • *London*

HarperCollins PUBLISHERS

4th Estate
An imprint of HarperCollins*Publishers*
1 London Bridge Street
London SE1 9GF
www.4thEstate.co.uk

First published in Great Britain in 2017 by 4th Estate
First published in the United States in 2017 by Alfred A. Knopf,
a division of Penguin Random House LLC

This is a slightly expanded version of a letter written by
the author as a Facebook post on 12 October 2016

2

Printed and bound in Great Britain by
Clays Ltd, St Ives plc

MIX
Paper from
responsible sources
FSC® C007454

FSC™ is a non-profit international organisation established to promote
the responsible management of the world's forests. Products carrying the
FSC label are independently certified to assure consumers that they come
from forests that are managed to meet the social, economic and
ecological needs of present and future generations,
and other controlled sources.

Find out more about HarperCollins and the environment at
www.harpercollins.co.uk/green

For Uju Egonu.
And for my baby sis, Ogechukwu Ikemelu.
With so much love.

Dear Ijeawele,

or

A Feminist Manifesto
in Fifteen Suggestions

Introduction

When a couple of years ago a friend of mine from childhood, who'd grown into a brilliant, strong, kind woman, asked me to tell her how to raise her baby girl a feminist, my first thought was that I did not know.

It felt like too huge a task.

But I had spoken publicly about feminism and perhaps that made her feel I was an expert on the subject. I had over the years also helped care for many babies of loved ones; I had worked as a babysitter and helped raise my nephews and nieces. I had done a lot of watching and listening, and I had done even more thinking.

In response to my friend's request, I decided to write her a letter, which I hoped would be honest and practical, while also serving as a map of sorts for my own feminist thinking. This book is a version of that letter, with some details changed.

Now that I, too, am the mother of a delightful baby girl, I realize how easy it is to dispense advice about raising a child when you are not facing the enormously complex reality of it yourself.

Still, I think it is morally urgent to have honest conversations about raising children differently, about trying to create a fairer world for women and men.

My friend sent me a reply saying she would 'try' to follow my suggestions.

And in rereading these as a mother, I too am determined to try.

Dear Ijeawele,

What joy. And what lovely names: Chizalum Adaora. She is so beautiful. Only a week old and she already looks curious about the world. What a magnificent thing you have done, bringing a human being into the world. 'Congratulations' feels too slight.

Your note made me cry. You know how I get foolishly emotional sometimes. Please know that I take your charge – how to raise her feminist – very seriously. And I understand what you mean by not always knowing what the feminist response to situations should be. For me, feminism is always contextual. I don't have a set-in-stone rule; the closest I have to a formula are my two 'Feminist Tools' and I want to share them with you as a starting point.

The first is your premise, the solid unbending belief that you start off with. What is your premise? Your feminist premise should be: I matter. I matter equally. Not 'if only'. Not 'as long as'. I matter equally. Full stop.

The second tool is a question: can you reverse X and get the same results?

For example: many people believe that a woman's feminist response to a husband's infidelity should be to leave. But I think staying can also be a feminist choice, depending on the context. If Chudi sleeps with another woman and you forgive him, would the same be true if you slept with another man? If the answer is yes, then your choosing to forgive him can be a feminist choice because it is not shaped by a gender inequality. Sadly, the reality in most marriages is that the answer to that question would often be no, and the reason would be gender-based – that absurd idea of 'men will be men', which means having a much lower standard for men.

I have some suggestions for how to raise Chizalum. But remember that you might do all the things I suggest, and she will still turn out to be different from what you hoped, because sometimes life just does its thing. What matters is that you try. And always trust your instincts above all else, because you will be guided by your love for your child.

Here are my suggestions:

First Suggestion

Be a full person. Motherhood is a glorious gift, but do not define yourself solely by motherhood. Be a full person. Your child will benefit from that. The pioneering American journalist Marlene Sanders, who was the first woman to report from Vietnam during the war (and who was the mother of a son), once gave this piece of advice to a younger journalist: 'Never apologize for working. You love what you do, and loving what you do is a great gift to give your child.'

I find this to be so wise and moving. You don't even have to love your job; you can merely love what your job does for you – the confidence and self-fulfilment that come with doing and earning.

It doesn't surprise me that your sister-in-law says you should be a 'traditional' mother and stay home, that Chudi can afford not to have a double-income family.

People will selectively use 'tradition' to justify anything. Tell her that a double-income family is actually the true Igbo tradition because not only did mothers farm and trade before British colonialism, trading was exclusively done by women in some parts of Igboland. She would know this if reading books were not such an alien enterprise to her. OK, that snark was to cheer you up. I know you are annoyed – and you should be – but it is really best to ignore her. Everybody will have an opinion about what you should do, but what matters is what you want for yourself, and not what others want you to want. Please reject the idea that motherhood and work are mutually exclusive.

Our mothers worked full-time while we were growing up, and we turned out well – at least you did; the jury is still out on me.

In these coming weeks of early motherhood, be kind to yourself. Ask for help. Expect to be helped. There is no such thing as a Superwoman. Parenting is about practice – and love. (I do wish, though, that 'parent' had not been turned into a verb, which I think is the root of the global middle-class phenomenon of 'parenting' as one endless, anxious journey of guilt.)

Give yourself room to fail. A new mother does not necessarily know how to calm a crying baby. Don't assume that you should know everything. Read books, look things up on the Internet, ask older parents, or just use trial and error. But above all, let your focus be on remaining a full person. Take time for yourself. Nurture your own needs.

Please do not think of it as 'doing it all'. Our culture celebrates the idea of women who are able to 'do it all' but does not question the premise of that praise. I have no interest in the debate about women 'doing it all' because it is a debate that assumes that care-giving and domestic work are singularly female domains, an idea that I strongly reject. Domestic work and care-giving should be gender-neutral, and we should be asking not whether a woman can 'do it all' but how best to support parents in their dual duties at work and at home.

Second Suggestion

Do it together. Remember in primary school we learned that a verb was a 'doing' word? Well, a father is as much a verb as a mother. Chudi should do everything that biology allows – which is everything but breastfeeding. Sometimes mothers, so conditioned to be all and do all, are complicit in diminishing the role of fathers. You might think that Chudi will not bathe her exactly as you'd like, that he might not wipe her bum as perfectly as you do. But so what? What is the worst that can happen? She won't die at the hands of her father. Seriously. He loves her. It's good for her to be cared for by her father. So look away, arrest your perfectionism, still your socially conditioned sense of duty. Share child care equally. 'Equally' of course depends on you both, and you will have to work it out, paying equal attention to each person's needs. It does not have to mean a literal fifty-fifty or a day-by-day score-keeping but you'll know when the child-care work is equally shared. You'll know by your lack of resentment. Because when there is true equality, resentment does not exist.

And please reject the language of help. Chudi is not 'helping' you by caring for his child. He is doing what he should. When we say fathers are 'helping', we are suggesting that child care is a mother's territory, into which fathers valiantly venture. It is not. Can you imagine how many more people today would be happier, more stable, better contributors to the world, if only their fathers had been actively present in their childhood? And never say that Chudi is 'babysitting' – people who babysit are people for whom the baby is not a primary responsibility.

Chudi does not deserve any special gratitude or praise, nor do you – you both made the choice to bring a child into the world, and the responsibility for that child belongs equally to you both. It would be different if you were a single mother, whether by circumstance or choice, because 'doing it together' would then not be an option. But you should not be a 'single mother' unless you are truly a single mother.

My friend Nwabu once told me that because his wife left when his kids were young, he became 'Mr Mum', by which he meant that he did the daily care-giving. But he was not being a 'Mr Mum'; he was simply being a dad.

Third Suggestion

Teach her that the idea of 'gender roles' is absolute nonsense. Do not ever tell her that she should or should not do something because she is a girl.

'Because you are a girl' is never a reason for anything. Ever.

I remember being told as a child to 'bend down properly while sweeping, like a girl'. Which meant that sweeping was about being female. I wish I had been told simply, 'bend down and sweep properly because you'll clean the floor better'. And I wish my brothers had been told the same thing.

There have been recent Nigerian social media debates about women and cooking, about how wives have to cook for husbands. It is funny, in the way that sad things are funny, that we are still talking about cooking as some kind of marriageability test for women.

The knowledge of cooking does not come pre-installed in a vagina. Cooking is learned. Cooking – domestic work in general – is a life skill that both men and women should ideally have. It is also a skill that can elude both men and women.

We also need to question the idea of marriage as a prize to women, because that is the basis of these absurd debates. If we stop conditioning women to see marriage as a prize, then we would have fewer debates about a wife needing to cook in order to earn that prize.

It is interesting to me how early the world starts to invent gender roles. Yesterday I went to a children's shop to buy Chizalum an outfit. In the girls' section were pale creations in washed-out shades of pink. I disliked them. The boys' section had outfits in vibrant shades of blue. Because I thought blue would be adorable against her brown skin – and photograph better – I bought one. At the checkout counter, the cashier said mine was the perfect present for the new boy. I said it was for a baby girl. She looked horrified. 'Blue for a girl?'

I cannot help but wonder about the clever marketing person who invented this pink-blue binary. There was also a 'gender-neutral' section, with its array of bloodless greys. 'Gender-neutral' is silly because it is premised on the idea of male being blue and female being pink and 'gender-neutral' being its own category. Why not just have baby clothes organized by age and displayed in all colours? The bodies of male and female infants are similar, after all.

I looked at the toy section, which was also arranged by gender. Toys for boys are mostly active, and involve some sort of doing – trains, cars – and toys for girls are mostly passive and are overwhelmingly dolls. I was struck by this. I had not quite realized how early society starts to invent ideas of what a boy should be and what a girl should be.

I wished the toys had been arranged by type, rather than by gender.

Did I ever tell you about going to a US mall with a seven-year-old Nigerian girl and her mother? She saw a toy helicopter, one of those things that fly by wireless remote control, and she was fascinated and asked for one. 'No,' her mother said. 'You have your dolls.' And she responded, 'Mummy, is it only dolls I will play with?'

I have never forgotten that. Her mother meant well, obviously. She was well versed in the ideas of gender roles – that girls play with dolls and boys with helicopters. I wonder now, wistfully, if the little girl would have turned out to be a revolutionary engineer, had she been given a chance to explore that helicopter.

If we don't place the straitjacket of gender roles on young children, we give them space to reach their full potential. Please see Chizalum as an individual. Not as a girl who should be a certain way. See her weaknesses and her strengths in an individual way. Do not measure her on a scale of what a girl should be. Measure her on a scale of being the best version of herself.

A young Nigerian woman once told me that she had for years behaved 'like a boy' – she liked football and was bored by dresses – until her mother forced her to stop her 'boyish' interests. Now she is grateful to her mother for helping her start behaving like a girl. The story made me sad. I wondered what parts of herself she had needed to silence and stifle, and I wondered about what her spirit had lost, because what she called 'behaving like a boy' was simply behaving like herself.

Another acquaintance, an American living in the Pacific Northwest, once told me that when she took her one-year-old son to a baby playgroup, where babies had been brought by their mothers, she noticed that the mothers of baby girls were very restraining, constantly telling the girls 'don't touch' or 'stop and be nice', and she noticed that the baby boys were encouraged to explore more and were not restrained as much and were almost never told to 'be nice'. Her theory was that parents unconsciously start very early to teach girls how to be, that baby girls are given less room and more rules and baby boys more room and fewer rules.

Gender roles are so deeply conditioned in us that we will often follow them even when they chafe against our true desires, our needs, our happiness. They are very difficult to unlearn, and so it is important to try to make sure that Chizalum rejects them from the beginning. Instead of letting her internalize the idea of gender roles, teach her self-reliance. Tell her that it is important to be able to do for herself and fend for herself. Teach her to try to fix physical things when they break. We are quick to assume girls can't do many things. Let her try. She might not fully succeed, but let her try. Buy her toys like blocks and trains – and dolls, too, if you want to.

Fourth Suggestion

Beware the danger of what I call Feminism Lite. It is the idea of conditional female equality. Please reject this entirely. It is a hollow, appeasing and bankrupt idea. Being a feminist is like being pregnant. You either are or you are not. You either believe in the full equality of men and women or you do not.

Feminism Lite uses analogies like 'he is the head and you are the neck'. Or 'he is driving but you are in the front seat'. More troubling is the idea, in Feminism Lite, that men are naturally superior but should be expected to 'treat women well'. No. No. No. There must be more than male benevolence as the basis for a woman's well-being.

Feminism Lite uses the language of 'allowing'. Theresa May is the British prime minister and here is how a progressive British newspaper described her husband: 'Philip May is known in politics as a man who has taken a back seat and allowed his wife, Theresa, to shine.'

Allowed.

Now let us reverse it. Theresa May has allowed her husband to shine. Does it make sense? If Philip May were prime minister, perhaps we might hear that his wife had 'supported' him from the background, or that she was 'behind' him, or that she'd 'stood by his side', but we would never hear that she had 'allowed' him to shine.

Allow is a troubling word. *Allow* is about power. You will often hear members of the Nigerian chapter of the Society of Feminism Lite say, 'Leave the woman alone to do what she wants as long as her husband allows.'

A husband is not a headmaster. A wife is not a schoolgirl. Permission and being allowed, when used one-sidedly – and they are nearly only used that way – should never be the language of an equal marriage.

Another egregious example of Feminism Lite: men who say 'Of course a wife does not always have to do the domestic work, I did domestic work when my wife travelled.'

Do you remember how we laughed and laughed at an atrociously written piece about me some years ago? The writer had accused me of being 'angry', as though 'being angry' were something to be ashamed of. Of course I am angry. I am angry about racism. I am angry about sexism. But I recently came to the realization that I am angrier about sexism than I am about racism.

Because in my anger about sexism, I often feel lonely. Because I love, and live among, many people who easily acknowledge race injustice but not gender injustice.

I cannot tell you how often people I care about – men and women – have expected me to make a case for sexism, to 'prove' it, as it were, while never having the same expectation for racism. (Obviously, in the wider world, too many people are still expected to 'prove' racism, but not in my close circle.) I cannot tell you how often people I care about have dismissed or diminished sexist situations.

Like our friend Ikenga, always quick to deny that anything is caused by misogyny, never interested in listening or engaging, always eager to explain how it is in fact women who are privileged. He once said, 'Even though the general idea is that my father is in charge at our home, it's my mother who is really in charge behind the scenes.' He thought he was refuting sexism, but he was making my case. Why 'behind the scenes'? If a woman has power then why do we need to disguise that she has power?

But here is a sad truth: our world is full of men and women who do not like powerful women. We have been so conditioned to think of power as male that a powerful woman is an aberration. And so she is policed. We ask of powerful women – is she humble? Does she smile? Is she grateful enough? Does she have a domestic side? Questions we do not ask of powerful men, which shows that our discomfort is not with power itself, but with women. We judge powerful women more harshly than we judge powerful men. And Feminism Lite enables this.

Fifth Suggestion

Teach Chizalum to read. Teach her to love books. The best way is by casual example. If she sees you reading, she will understand that reading is valuable. If she were not to go to school, and merely just read books, she would arguably become more knowledgeable than a conventionally educated child. Books will help her understand and question the world, help her express herself, and help her in whatever she wants to become – a chef, a scientist, a singer, all benefit from the skills that reading brings. I do not mean school books. I mean books that have nothing to do with school, autobiographies and novels and histories. If all else fails, pay her to read. Reward her. I know this remarkable Nigerian woman, Angela, a single mother who was raising her child in the United States; her child did not take to reading so she decided to pay her five cents per page. An expensive endeavour, she later joked, but a worthy investment.

Sixth Suggestion

Teach her to question language. Language is the repository of our prejudices, our beliefs, our assumptions. But to teach her that, you will have to question your own language. A friend of mine says she will never call her daughter 'princess'. People mean well when they say this, but 'princess' is loaded with assumptions, of a girl's delicacy, of the prince who will come to save her, etc. This friend prefers 'angel' and 'star'.

So decide for yourself the things you will not say to your child. Because what you say to your child matters. It teaches her what she should value. You know that Igbo joke, used to tease girls who are being childish – 'What are you doing? Don't you know you are old enough to find a husband?' I used to say that often. But now I choose not to. I say, 'You are old enough to find a job.' Because I do not believe that marriage is something we should teach young girls to aspire to.

Try not to use words like 'misogyny' and 'patriarchy' too often with Chizalum. We feminists can sometimes be too jargony, and jargon can sometimes feel too abstract. Don't just label something misogynistic; tell her why it is, and tell her what would make it not be.

Teach her that if you criticize X in women but do not criticize X in men, then you do not have a problem with X, you have a problem with women. For X please insert words like anger, ambition, loudness, stubbornness, coldness, ruthlessness.

Teach her to ask questions like: what are the things that women cannot do because they are women? Do these things have cultural prestige? If so, why are only men allowed to do the things that have cultural prestige?

It is helpful, I think, to use everyday examples.

Remember that television commercial we watched in Lagos, where a man cooks and his wife claps for him? True progress is when she doesn't clap for him but just reacts to the food itself – she can either praise the food or not praise the food, just as he can praise hers or not praise hers, but what is sexist is that she is praising the fact that he has undertaken the act of cooking, praise that implies that cooking is an inherently female act.

Remember the mechanic in Lagos who was described as a 'lady mechanic' in a newspaper profile? Teach Chizalum that the woman is a mechanic, not a 'lady mechanic'.

Point out to her how wrong it is that a man who hits your car in Lagos traffic gets out and tells you to go and bring your husband because he 'can't deal with a woman'.

Instead of merely telling her, show her with examples that misogyny can be overt and misogyny can be subtle and that both are abhorrent.

Teach her to question men who can have empathy for women only if they see them as relational rather than as individual equal humans. Men who, when discussing rape, will always say something like 'if it were my daughter or wife or sister'. Yet such men do not need to imagine a male victim of crime as a brother or son in order to feel empathy. Teach her, too, to question the idea of women as a special species. I once heard an American politician, in his bid to show his support for women, speak of how women should be 'revered' and 'championed' – a sentiment that is all too common.

Tell Chizalum that women actually don't need to be championed and revered; they just need to be treated as equal human beings. There is a patronizing undertone to the idea of women needing to be 'championed and revered' because they are women. It makes me think of chivalry, and the premise of chivalry is female weakness.

Seventh Suggestion

Never speak of marriage as an achievement. Find ways to make clear to her that marriage is not an achievement, nor is it what she should aspire to. A marriage can be happy or unhappy, but it is not an achievement.

We condition girls to aspire to marriage and we do not condition boys to aspire to marriage, and so there is already a terrible imbalance at the start. The girls will grow up to be women preoccupied with marriage. The boys will grow up to be men who are not preoccupied with marriage. The women marry those men. The relationship is automatically uneven because the institution matters more to one than the other. Is it any wonder that, in so many marriages, women sacrifice more, at a loss to themselves, because they have to constantly maintain an uneven exchange? One consequence of this imbalance is the very shabby and very familiar phenomenon of two women publicly fighting over a man, while the man remains silent.

When Hillary Clinton was running for president of the United States, the first descriptor on her Twitter account was 'Wife'. The first descriptor on the Twitter account of Bill Clinton, her husband, is 'Founder', not 'Husband'. (Because of this, I have an unreasonable affection for the very few men who use 'husband' as their first descriptor.) In a strange way, it doesn't feel unusual that she would define herself as a wife like this, while he doesn't define himself as a husband. It feels normal, because it is so common; our world still largely values a woman's marital and maternal roles more than anything else.

After she married Bill Clinton in 1975, Hillary Clinton kept her name, Hillary

Rodham. Eventually she began to add his name, Clinton, to hers and then after a while she dropped Rodham because of political pressure – because her husband would lose voters who were offended that his wife had kept her name.

Reading of this made me think not only of how American voters apparently place retrograde marital expectations on women, but also of my own experience with my name.

You remember how a journalist unilaterally decided to give me a new name – Mrs Husband's Surname – on learning that I was married, and how I asked him to stop because that was not my name. I will never forget the smouldering hostility from some Nigerian women in response to this. It is interesting that there was more hostility, in general, from women (than from men), many of whom insisted on calling me what was not my name, as though to silence my voice.

I wondered about that, and thought that perhaps for many of them, my choice represented a challenge to their idea of what is the norm.

Even some friends made statements like: 'You are successful and so it is OK to keep your name.' Which made me wonder: why does a woman have to be successful at work in order to justify keeping her name?

The truth is that I have not kept my name because I am successful. Had I not had the good fortune to be published and widely read, I would still have kept my name. I have kept my name because it is my name. I have kept my name because I like my name.

There are people who say, 'Well, your name is also about patriarchy because it is your father's name.' Indeed. But the point is simply this: whether it came from my father or from the moon, it is the name that I have had since I was born, the name with which I travelled my life's milestones, the name I have answered to since that first day I went to kindergarten in Nsukka on a hazy morning and my teacher said, 'Answer "present" if you hear your name. Number one: Adichie!'

More important, every woman should have the choice of keeping her name – but the reality is that there is an overwhelming societal pressure to conform. There are obviously women who want to take their husband's name, but there are women who do not want to conform yet for whom the required energy – mental, emotional, even physical – is just too much. How many men do you think would be willing to change their name on getting married?

'Mrs' is a title I dislike because Nigerian society gives it too much value. I have observed too many cases of men and women who proudly speak of the title of Mrs as though those who are not Mrs have somehow failed at something. Mrs can be a choice, but to infuse it with as much value as our culture does is disturbing. The value we give to Mrs means that marriage changes the social status of a woman but not that of a man. (Is that perhaps why many women complain of married men still 'acting' as though they were single? Perhaps if our society asked married men to change their names and take on a new title, different from Mr, their behaviour might change as well? Ha!) But more seriously, if you, a twenty-eight-year-old master's degree holder, go overnight from Ijeawele Eze to Mrs Ijeawele Udegbunam, surely it requires not just the mental energy of changing passports and licences but also a psychic change, a new 'becoming'? This new 'becoming' would not matter so much if men, too, had to undergo it.

I prefer Ms because it is similar to Mr. A man is Mr whether married or not, a woman is Ms whether married or not. So please teach Chizalum that in a truly just society, women should not be expected to make marriage-based changes that men are not expected to make. Here's a nifty solution: each couple that marries should take on an entirely new surname, chosen however they want as long as both agree to it, so that a day after the wedding, both husband and wife can hold hands and joyfully journey off to the municipal offices to change their passports, driver's licences, signatures, initials, bank accounts, etc.

Eighth Suggestion

Teach her to reject likeability. Her job is not to make herself likeable, her job is to be her full self, a self that is honest and aware of the equal humanity of other people. Remember I told you how upsetting it was to me that our friend Chioma would often tell me that 'people' would not 'like' something I wanted to say or do? I always felt, from her, the unspoken pressure to change myself to fit some mould that would please an amorphous entity called 'people'. It was upsetting because we want those close to us to encourage us to be our most authentic selves.

Please do not ever put this pressure on your daughter. We teach girls to be likeable, to be nice, to be false. And we do not teach boys the same. This is dangerous. Many sexual predators have capitalized on this. Many girls remain silent when abused because they want to be nice. Many girls spend too much time trying to be 'nice' to people who do them harm. Many girls think of the 'feelings' of those who are hurting them. This is the catastrophic consequence of likeability. We have a world full of women who are unable to exhale fully because they have for so long been conditioned to fold themselves into shapes to make themselves likeable.

So instead of teaching Chizalum to be likeable, teach her to be honest. And kind.

And brave. Encourage her to speak her mind, to say what she really thinks, to speak truthfully. And then praise her when she does. Praise her especially when she takes a stand that is difficult or unpopular because it happens to be her honest position. Tell her that kindness matters. Praise her when she is kind to other people. But teach her that her kindness must never be taken for granted. Tell her that she too deserves the kindness of others. Teach her to stand up for what is hers. If another child takes her toy without her permission, ask her to take it back, because her consent is important. Tell her that if anything ever makes her uncomfortable, to speak up, to say it, to shout.

Show her that she does not need to be liked by everyone. Tell her that if someone does not like her, there *will* be someone else who will. Teach her that she is not merely an object to be liked or disliked, she is also a subject who can like or dislike. In her teenage years, if she comes home crying about some boys who don't like her, let her know she can choose not to like those boys – yes, it's hard, I know, just remembering my crush on Nnamdi in secondary school.

But still I wish somebody had told me this.

Ninth Suggestion

Give Chizalum a sense of identity. It matters. Be deliberate about it. Let her grow up to think of herself as, among other things, a proud Igbo woman. And you must be selective – teach her to embrace the parts of Igbo culture that are beautiful and teach her to reject the parts that are not. You can say to her, in different contexts and different ways, 'Igbo culture is lovely because it values community and consensus and hard work, and the language and proverbs are beautiful and full of great wisdom. But Igbo culture also teaches that a woman cannot do certain things just because she's a woman and that is wrong. Igbo culture also focuses a little too much on materialism, and while money is important – because money means self-reliance – you must not value people based on who has money and who does not.'

Be deliberate also about showing her the enduring beauty and resilience of Africans and of black people. Why? Because of the power dynamics in the world, she will grow up seeing images of white beauty, white ability and white achievement, no matter where she is in the world. It will be in the TV shows she watches, in the popular culture she consumes, in the books she reads. She will also probably grow up seeing many negative images of blackness and of Africans.

Teach her to take pride in the history of Africans, and in the black diaspora. Find black heroes, men and women, in history. They exist. You might have to counter some of the things she will learn in school – the Nigerian curriculum isn't quite infused with the idea of teaching children to have a sense of pride in their history. So her teachers will be fantastic at teaching her mathematics and science and art and music, but you will have to do the pride-teaching yourself.

Teach her about privilege and inequality and the importance of giving dignity to every-one who does not mean her harm – teach her that the household help is human just like her, teach her always to greet the driver. Link these expectations to her identity – for example, say to her, 'In our family, when you are a child, you greet those older than you no matter what job they do.'

Give her an Igbo nickname. When I was growing up, my Aunty Gladys called me Ada Obodo Dike. I always loved that. Apparently my village, Ezi-Abba, is known as the Land of Warriors and to be called Daughter of the Land of Warriors was deliciously heady.

Tenth Suggestion

Be deliberate about how you engage with her and her appearance.

Encourage her participation in sports. Teach her to be physically active. Take walks with her. Swim. Run. Play tennis. Football. Table tennis. All kinds of sports. Any kind of sports. I think this is important not only because of the obvious health benefits but because it can help with all the body-image insecurities that the world thrusts on girls. Let Chizalum know that there is great value in being active. Studies show that girls generally stop playing sports as puberty arrives. Not surprising. Breasts and self-consciousness can get in the way of sports – I stopped playing football when my breasts first appeared because all I wanted to do was hide the existence of my breasts, and running and tackling didn't help. Please try not to let that get in her way.

If she likes make-up, let her wear it. If she likes fashion, let her dress up. But if she doesn't like either, let her be. Don't think that raising her feminist means forcing her to reject femininity. Feminism and femininity are not mutually exclusive. It is misogynistic to suggest that they are. Sadly, women have learned to be ashamed and apologetic about pursuits that are seen as traditionally female, such as fashion and make-up. But our society does not expect men to feel ashamed of pursuits considered generally male – sports cars, certain professional sports. In the same way, men's grooming is never suspect in the way women's grooming is – a well-dressed man does not worry that, because he is dressed well, certain assumptions might be made about his intelligence, his ability, or his seriousness. A woman, on the other hand, is always aware of how a bright lipstick or a carefully put-together outfit might very well make others assume her to be frivolous.

Never ever link Chizalum's appearance with morality. Never tell her that a short skirt is 'immoral'. Make dressing a question of taste and attractiveness instead of a question of morality. If you both clash over what she wants to wear, never say things like 'You look like a prostitute', as I know your mother once told you. Instead say: 'That dress doesn't flat-ter you like this other one.' Or doesn't fit as well. Or doesn't look as attractive. Or is simply ugly. But never 'immoral'. Because clothes have absolutely nothing to do with morality.

Try not to link hair with pain. I think of my childhood and how often I cried while my dense long hair was being plaited. I think of how a packet of Smarties was kept in front of me as a reward if I sat through having my hair done. And for what? Imagine if we had not spent so many Saturdays of our childhood and teenagehood doing our hair. What might we have learned? In what ways might we have grown? What did boys do on Saturdays?

So with her hair, I suggest that you redefine 'neat'. Part of the reason that hair is about pain for so many girls is that adults are determined to conform to a version of 'neat' that means Too Tight and Scalp-Destroying and Headache-Infusing.

We need to stop. I've seen girls in school in Nigeria being terribly harassed for their hair not being 'neat', merely because some of their God-given hair had curled up in glorious tight little balls at their temples. Make Chizalum's hair loose – big plaits and big cornrows, and don't use a tiny-toothed comb that wasn't made with our hair texture in mind.

And make that your definition of neat. Go to her school and talk to the administration if you have to. It takes one person to make change happen.

Chizalum will notice very early on – because children are perceptive – what kind of beauty the mainstream world values. She will see it in magazines and films and television. She will see that whiteness is valued. She will notice that the hair texture that is valued is straight or swingy, and hair that is valued falls down rather than stands up. She will encounter these values whether you like it or not. So make sure that you create alternatives for her to see. Let her know that slim white women are beautiful, and that non-slim, non-white women are beautiful. Let her know that there are many individuals and many cultures that do not find the narrow mainstream definition of beauty attractive. You will know your child best, and so you will know best how to affirm her own kind of beauty, how to protect her from looking at her own reflection with dissatisfaction.

Surround her with a village of aunties, women who have qualities you'd like her to admire. Talk about how much you admire them. Children copy and learn from example. Talk about what you admire about them. I, for example, particularly admire the African American feminist Florynce Kennedy. Some African women that I would tell her about are Ama Ata Aidoo, Dora Akunyili, Muthoni Likimani, Ngozi Okonjo-Iweala, Taiwo Ajai-Lycett. There are so many African women who are sources of feminist inspiration. Because of what they have done and because of what they have refused to do. Like your grandmother, by the way, that remarkable, strong, sharp-tongued babe.

Surround Chizalum, too, with a village of uncles. This will be harder, judging from the kind of friends Chudi has. I still cannot get over that blustering man with the over-carved beard who kept saying at Chudi's last birthday party, 'Any woman I marry cannot tell me what to do!!'

So please find some good non-blustering men. Men like your brother Ugomba, men like our friend Chinakueze. Because the truth is that she will encounter a lot of male bluster in her life. So it is good to have alternatives from very early on.

I cannot overstate the power of alternatives. She can counter ideas about static 'gender roles' if she has been empowered by her familiarity with alternatives. If she knows an uncle who cooks well – and does so with indifference – then she can smile and brush off the foolishness of somebody who claims that 'women must do the cooking'.

Eleventh Suggestion

Teach her to question our culture's selective use of biology as 'reasons' for social norms.

I know a Yoruba woman, married to an Igbo man, who was pregnant with her first child and was thinking of first names for the child. All the names were Igbo.

Shouldn't her children have Yoruba first names since they would have their father's Igbo surname? I asked, and she said, 'A child first belongs to the father. It has to be that way.'

We often use biology to explain the privileges that men have, the most common reason being men's physical superiority. It is of course true that men are in general physically stronger than women. But if we truly depended on biology as the root of social norms, then children would be identified as their mother's rather than their father's because when a child is born, the parent we are biologically – and incontrovertibly – certain of is the mother. We assume the father is who the mother says the father is. How many lineages all over the world are not biological, I wonder?

For many Igbo women, the conditioning is so complete that women think of children *only* as the father's. I know of women who have left bad marriages but not been 'allowed' to take their children or even to see their children because the children belong to the man.

We also use evolutionary biology to explain male promiscuity, but not to explain female promiscuity, even though it really makes evolutionary sense for women to have many sexual partners – the larger the genetic pool, the greater will be the chances of bearing offspring who will thrive.

So teach Chizalum that biology is an interesting and fascinating subject, but she should never accept it as justification for any social norm. Because social norms are created by human beings, and there is no social norm that cannot be changed.

Twelfth Suggestion

Talk to her about sex, and start early. It will probably be a bit awkward but it is necessary.

Remember that seminar we went to in class 3 where we were supposed to be taught about 'sexuality' but instead we listened to vague semi-threats about how 'talking to boys' would end up with us being pregnant and disgraced? I remember that hall and that seminar as a place filled with shame. Ugly shame. The particular brand of shame that has to do with being female. May your daughter never encounter it.

With her, don't pretend that sex is merely a controlled act of reproduction. Or an 'only in marriage' act, because that is disingenuous. (You and Chudi were having sex long before marriage and she will probably know this by the time she is twelve.) Tell her that sex can be a beautiful thing and that, apart from the obvious physical consequences (for her as the woman!), it can also have emotional consequences. Tell her that her body belongs to her and her alone, that she should never feel the need to say yes to something she does not want, or something she feels pressured to do. Teach her that saying no when no feels right is something to be proud of.

Tell her you think it's best to wait until she is an adult before she has sex. But be prepared because she might not wait until she's eighteen. And if she doesn't wait, you have to make sure she is able to tell you that she hasn't.

It's not enough to say you want to raise a daughter who can tell you anything; you have to give her the language to talk to you. And I mean this in a literal way. What should she call it? What word should she use?

I remember people used 'ike' when I was a child to mean both 'anus' and 'vagina'; 'anus' was the easier meaning but it left everything vague and I never quite knew how to say, for example, that I had an itch in my vagina.

Most childhood development experts say it is best to have children call sexual organs by their proper biological names – vagina and penis. I agree, but that is a decision you have to make. You should decide what name you want her to call it, but what matters is that there must be a name and that it cannot be a name that is weighed down with shame.

To make sure she doesn't inherit shame from you, you have to free yourself of your own inherited shame. And I know how terribly difficult that is. In every culture in the world, female sexuality is about shame. Even cultures that expect women to be sexy – like many in the West – still do not expect them to be sexual.

The shame we attach to female sexuality is about control. Many cultures and religions control women's bodies in one way or another. If the justification for controlling women's bodies were about women themselves, then it would be understandable. If, for example, the reason was 'women should not wear short skirts because they can get cancer if they do'. Instead the reason is not about women, but about men. Women must be 'covered up' to protect men. I find this deeply dehumanizing because it reduces women to mere props used to manage the appetites of men.

And speaking of shame – never, ever link sexuality and shame. Or nakedness and shame. Do not ever make 'virginity' a focus. Every conversation about virginity becomes a conversation about shame. Teach her to reject the linking of shame and female biology. Why were we raised to speak in low tones about periods? To be filled with shame if our menstrual blood happened to stain our skirt? Periods are nothing to be ashamed of. Periods are normal and natural, and the human species would not be here if periods did not exist. I remember a man who said a period was like shit. Well, sacred shit, I told him, because you wouldn't be here if periods didn't happen.

Thirteenth Suggestion

Romance will happen, so be on board.

I'm writing this assuming she is heterosexual – she might not be, obviously. But I am assuming that because it is what I feel best equipped to talk about.

Make sure you are aware of the romance in her life. And the only way you can do that is to start very early to give her the language with which to talk to you not only about sex but also about love. I don't mean you should be her 'friend'; I mean you should be her mother to whom she can talk about everything.

Teach her that to love is not only to give but also to take. This is important because we give girls subtle cues about their lives – we teach girls that a large component of their ability to love is their ability to sacrifice their selves. We do not teach this to boys. Teach her that to love she must give of herself emotionally but she must also expect to be given to.

I think love is the most important thing in life. Whatever kind, however you define it, but I think of it generally as being greatly valued by another human being and greatly valuing another human being. But why do we raise only one half of the world to value this? I was recently in a roomful of young women and was struck by how much of the conversation was about men – what terrible things men had done to them, this man cheated, this man lied, this man promised marriage and disappeared, this husband did this and that.

And I realized, sadly, that the reverse is not true. A roomful of men do not invariably end up talking about women – and if they do, it is more likely to be in flippant terms rather than as lamentations of life. Why?

It goes back, I think, to that early conditioning. At a recent baby's baptism ceremony, guests were asked to write their wishes for the baby girl. One guest wrote: 'I wish for you a good husband.' Well-intentioned but very troubling. A three-month-old baby girl already being told that a husband is something to aspire to. Had the baby been a boy, it would not have occurred to that guest to wish for him 'a good wife'.

And speaking of women lamenting about men who 'promise' marriage and then disappear – isn't it odd that in most societies in the world today, women generally cannot propose marriage? Marriage is such a major step in your life and yet you cannot take charge of it; it depends on a man asking you. So many women are in long-term relationships and want to get married but have to wait for the man to propose – and often this waiting becomes a performance, sometimes unconscious and sometimes not, of marriage-worthiness. If we apply the first Feminism Tool here, then it makes no sense that a woman who matters equally has to wait for somebody else to initiate what will be a major life change for her.

A Feminism Lite adherent once told me that the fact that our society expects men to make proposals proves that women have the power, because only if a woman says yes can marriage happen. The truth is this – the real power resides in the person who asks. Before you can say yes or no, you first must be asked. I truly wish for Chizalum a world in which either person can propose, in which a relationship has become so comfortable, so joy-filled, that whether or not to embark on marriage becomes a conversation, itself filled with joy.

I want to say something about money here. Teach her never ever to say such nonsense as 'my money is my money and his money is our money'. It is vile. And dangerous – to have that attitude means that you must potentially accept other harmful ideas as well. Teach her that it is NOT a man's role to provide. In a healthy relationship, it is the role of whoever can provide to provide.

Fourteenth Suggestion

In teaching her about oppression, be careful not to turn the oppressed into saints. Saintliness is not a prerequisite for dignity. People who are unkind and dishonest are still human, and still deserve dignity. Property rights for rural Nigerian women, for example, is a major feminist issue, and the women do not need to be good and angelic to be allowed their property rights.

There is sometimes, in the discourse around gender, the assumption that women are supposed to be morally 'better' than men. They are not. Women are as human as men are. Female goodness is as normal as female evil.

And there are many women in the world who do not like other women. Female misogyny exists, and to evade acknowledging it is to create unnecessary opportunities for anti-feminists to try to discredit feminism. I mean the sort of anti-feminists who will gleefully raise examples of women saying 'I am not a feminist' as though a person born with a vagina making this statement somehow automatically discredits feminism. That a woman claims not to be feminist does not diminish the necessity of feminism. If anything, it makes us see the extent of the problem, the successful reach of patriarchy. It shows us, too, that not all women are feminists and not all men are misogynists.

Fifteenth Suggestion

Teach her about difference. Make difference ordinary. Make difference normal. Teach her not to attach value to difference. And the reason for this is not to be fair or to be nice but merely to be human and practical. Because difference is the reality of our world. And by teaching her about difference, you are equipping her to survive in a diverse world.

She must know and understand that people walk different paths in the world and that as long as those paths do no harm to others, they are valid paths that she must respect. Teach her that we do not know – we cannot know – everything about life. Both religion and science have spaces for the things we do not know, and it is enough to make peace with that.

Teach her never to universalize her own standards or experiences. Teach her that her standards are for her alone, and not for other people. This is the only necessary form of humility: the realization that difference is normal.

Tell her that some people are gay, and some are not. A little child has two daddies or two mummies because some people just do. Tell her that some people go to mosque and others go to church and others go to different places of worship and still others don't worship at all, because that is just the way it is for some people.

You say to her: You like palm oil but some people don't like palm oil.

She says to you: Why?

You say to her: I don't know. It's just the way the world is.

Please note that I am not suggesting that you raise her to be 'non-judgemental', which is a commonly used expression these days, and which slightly worries me. The general sentiment behind the idea is a fine one, but 'non-judgemental' can easily devolve into meaning 'don't have an opinion about anything' or 'I keep my opinions to myself'. And so, instead of that, what I hope for Chizalum is this: that she will be full of opinions, and that her opinions will come from an informed, humane and broad-minded place.

May she be healthy and happy. May her life be whatever she wants it to be.

Do you have a headache after reading all this? Sorry. Next time don't ask me how to raise your daughter feminist.

With love, oyi gi,
Chimamanda

About the Author

Chimamanda Ngozi Adichie grew up in Nigeria. Her work has been translated into thirty languages and has appeared in various publications, including *The New Yorker*, *Granta*, *The O. Henry Prize Stories*, the *Financial Times* and *Zoetrope: All-Story*. She is the author of the novels *Purple Hibiscus*, which won the Commonwealth Writers' Prize and the Hurston/Wright Legacy Award; *Half of a Yellow Sun*, which won the Orange Prize and was a National Book Critics Circle Award finalist, a *New York Times* Notable Book, and a *People* and *Black Issues Book Review* Best Book of the Year; *Americanah*, which won the

National Book Critics Circle Award and was a *New York Times*, *Washington Post*, *Chicago Tribune* and *Entertainment Weekly* Best Book of the Year; the story collection *The Thing Around Your Neck*; and the essay *We Should All Be Feminists*. A recipient of a MacArthur Fellowship, she divides her time between the United States and Nigeria.

www.chimamanda.com
www.facebook.com/chimamandaadichie